The DIY Blacksmithing Book

by Terran Marks

You can get started blacksmithing today at diyblacksmithing.teachable.com!

Table of Contents

Why We're Here

There is no shortage of information about blacksmithing and metalworking out there.

With the Internet, we have access to more useful (and not-so-useful) information than ever before.

What is lacking is a consolidation of the basics of do-it-yourself blacksmithing. With this book I aim to change that.

Hello! My name is Terran Marks and I am a professional blacksmith. I learned the trade at the John C. Campbell Folk School in North Carolina and I've been smitten ever since.

I love the craft and I love talking about it. I love it so much I created a website about it when I was first starting out.

The site, **DIY Blacksmithing**, started out as a simple documentation of what it was like for me setting up my forge, buying my first hammer, and selling my first hook.

Over the years the site has expanded to include a variety of tools and resources for thousands of blacksmiths around the world.

One of the most popular tools to date is the Find a Blacksmithing School Map. My goal was to make it as easy as possible for people to find blacksmithing classes near them.

So, I created an interactive map that allows you to click on any state in the U.S. to find a list of blacksmith schools for that state.

I apologize if I'm starting to run off on a tangent. What I'm getting at is that I enjoy gathering information and sharing it with other blacksmiths. Seeing people take steps toward their goals and being a small part of that process is gratifying.

That brings us to **my philosophy on blacksmithing**:

Anyone can set up a blacksmith shop with the right information and a clearly laid-out plan.

It has always helped me accomplish things when a complex task is laid out in steps. This "chunking" helps me focus on the smaller parts of a larger goal.

Throughout this book I'll be breaking down each step of the blacksmithing process into smaller, more manageable pieces.

At the end of each chapter you will find a "Next Steps Checklist" that you can use to track your progress toward your blacksmithing goals.

I will also be giving examples from my own experiences as well as hypothetical scenarios to illustrate various aspects of blacksmithing.

I hope The DIY Blacksmithing Book becomes a valuable resource for you as you

continue down this path.

CHAPTER ONE:

Initial Costs

Let's get the money discussion out of the way first thing so we can relax as we go deeper into the material. Here's the big hairy question:

How much do you have to spend?

Thankfully, the answer is **not very much**. What I'll do in this chapter is lay out the bare minimum you will need in terms of equipment to get forging as soon as possible. In the following chapters I'll get into the nitty-gritty of each aspect in the list below.

Here is a list of what you will need and their associated costs:

-Hammer: $0-$110 average $30

-Tongs: $0-$40

-Anvil: $30-$1000+

-Forge: $30-$800+

-Rent: $0-$1000+

-Metal: $0.50-$100+

As you will see throughout this book, there are inexpensive ways to start forging. There are also some very expensive ways to start. My goal is to show the least expensive way and explain why that's not always the easiest way.

Hammer

I started with a $27 cross peen blacksmith's hammer purchased on Amazon. It's nothing fancy, but it has all the features you need starting out. You can find brand and size details on The DIY Blacksmithing site (http:// diyblacksmith.blogspot.com).

Tongs

Next, I would go to the Blacksmith Supply website and pick out one or two pairs of tongs. The bolt style Tom Tongs I like to use cost between $35 and $40. I have used this style to create hooks, pot racks, fire rakes, punches, candelabras, and wall brackets of all sizes.

Anvil

The first place I would look is on eBay. You are likely to find quite a few sellers offering pieces of railroad track and Harbor Freight ASOs (Anvil-shaped Objects). Avoid the ASOs, but definitely consider a piece of track as an inexpensive option. For $30 you can get started.

If you would like to do some more legwork, take a look at Craigslist in your area. You can use the search box on the left side of the Craigslist page for your area to find anvils for sale.

There are also the traditional options: talking to local folks and looking around at flea markets, estate sales, and swap meets.

Forge

The least expensive way to solve the forge problem is to build your own. You can do this with an old charcoal grill, some pipe, and a hairdryer. The details of this set-up are laid out in the chapter on **Forges**.

Rent

If you have space in your backyard, you're all set. I'll show you a set-up I built over a weekend in the Creating Your Workspace chapter.

If you don't have space in your backyard or you're loving the city life, you will have to get creative. Look into art schools in your area, shared workspaces for creative people, industrial areas with space to rent, and rental properties outside the city limits.

Note: Most cities have noise ordinances that require you to silence the racket between certain nighttime hours. Look into your local jurisdiction to find out exactly when you can beat on metal.

Another option is to contact one of the blacksmithing schools in your state. The nice folks at your local school will likely have some great ideas for where to set up.

To make it easier to find schools, I created a map that's free to use on The DIY Blacksmithing site (http://diyblacksmith.blogspot.com).

Metal

You can spend your Saturdays riffling through the local scrap yard and come up with pure gold. Old leaf springs and piston arms are just some of the good metal you can find.

If you want metal with specific characteristics, you can find many metal suppliers online. Speedy Metals is a great source. Even Amazon can get you set up with mild steel, o1 tool steel, or whatever you like.

GRAND TOTAL

Conservatively, I believe that you can get set up for $150 depending on a few things:

- You have the space to set up your work area.

- You have the time to search around for the right tools at the right price.

- You don't mind exercising your ingenuity to make things come together.

However, if you're in a hurry to start forging, paying a little extra money upfront can go a long way. In the following chapters, we'll go through your options together.

CHAPTER TWO:

Metal

Unlike goldsmiths, silversmiths, and even fine woodworkers, our raw materials are pretty darn cheap. You can easily pick up 12 inches of freshly manufactured 0.50" diameter mild steel for less than $2.00 and make a set of hooks that sells for $30.

In this chapter, we'll talk about commonly used types of steel and the various places you can find them. At the end of the chapter you will find a **Next Steps Checklist** to follow to find a great steel supplier.

Steel Types

First, a primer on common types of steel to speed up your selection process. You could make just about any item out of any type of steel, but certain grades of steel are more suitable for certain things.

For example, you can make a knife out of mild steel, but it's going to be soft and won't last long. What you will end up with is a knife-shaped piece of very sharp metal. While this *is* a great way to practice before using tool steel, it's not what you want for your final product.

You also don't want to spend hours wailing away on a piece of tool steel just to make a decorative wall hook. You certainly could, but mild steel is durable and strong enough to hold up most items.

Now let's get into the common types of steel.

Mild Steel

This is the main type of steel most people start with. It's the least expensive and easiest to work due to its lower carbon content.

When we're talking about carbon content, we're referring to the percentage of carbon present in the steel. Carbon in steel gives the material its strength, but if the carbon content is high, the piece will require more work to bend and shape.

Low carbon content mild steel is what I use most often to create wall hooks and other household items. The two most common types are **1018** and **1045**.

1018 is good for lots of different applications. In more industrial settings it can be used for machine parts, tool and die sets, pinions, and gears. Something to keep in mind is that it can crack under extreme or repeated bending.

1045 is more durable than 1018 and other lower carbon steels. It is slightly more expensive, but we're only talking about $1 more at most for a piece of steel of the same dimensions.

High Carbon or Tool Steel

To oversimplify, "high carbon" means that the steel is much harder than mild steel. It's suitable for tool making, knife making, and forging structural elements. This is what you're getting when you harvest steel from the leaf springs of cars or old railroad spikes. It is made to withstand greater forces than mild steel and to be more durable.

If you're buying straight from a manufacturer, the grade to ask for is **A2** as it comes in round and square stock.

If knife making is something you would like to experiment with, you can find pieces of O1 steel (that's "O" as in Oscar) that are 18 inches long for around $30 on Amazon.

If you come across a steel supplier you like, you should ask them about the other grades of tool steel. Some of my most informative conversations have been about types of steel and their uses. I'm sure they would be happy to talk to you about their applications.

Note: Tool steel tends to be more expensive than mild steel. For comparison, the same 12 *inch piece of 1045 grade 0.50" round mild steel will cost half the amount of a 12 inch piece of A2 tool steel. This isn't a firm ratio. Always do your due diligence for cost comparisons.*

Hot Rolled vs. Cold Finished Steel

While you are searching around for material, you are likely to come across these two terms. Here is a quick way to differentiate between them.

Hot rolled steel is rolled and shaped while it's still hot. Because of this it has to cool down. This cooling process results in a rougher, oxidized surface. It generally has higher carbon content and is harder to work. On the plus side, it is often cheaper than cold finished steel of the same dimensions.

Cold finished steel (also often referred to as cold rolled) is a smoother product and easier to work with. It is rolled out and shaped while it's cold so the oxidation of the material doesn't occur.

For my money, I usually buy cold finished mild steel.

Hopefully this hasn't made steel selection more complicated. When you're just getting started I don't want you to sweat these finer points too much.

WHERE TO GET IT

Steel Suppliers

In the United States, it's fairly easy to find steel suppliers in larger cities. I've lived in multiple states over the years and have never been more than an hour or two away from a steel supplier.

For example, I'm from a small town in southern Indiana. Within 30 minutes I have a handful of scrap yards as well as a genuine steel supplier.

When I lived in Seattle I used Everett Steel exclusively. The folks who staff the Seattle site are very friendly and love small business owners.

These are just a couple of examples to give you some ideas. With access to the Internet, finding a local source for steel is pretty straightforward.

Some helpful search terms are:

"steel suppliers + your town or city name"

"steel by the foot + city name"

I listed steel suppliers first, but they aren't necessarily the cheapest or most convenient. Next, we'll talk about two options that might suit you better.

Scrap yards

Take a Saturday and go talk to the folks down at the scrap yard. They're almost always buying and selling all types of metal. You're likely to get a deal, too.

Pro Tip: Go in with some idea of what you want. The scrap yard is good place to find car leaf springs and other tool grade steel.

Online

Living in a steel desert with no suppliers to be found? You can order a variety of grades of steel to length online.

Speedy Metals has a huge selection of different grades with clear descriptions detailing their uses. This is a great resource for learning more about different types of metal in general including brass, copper, and galvanized.

Metal by the Foot is another site that has an easy to use homepage with selection drop-down boxes. Prices are comparable to Speedy Metals.

If you would rather not add your credit card information to yet another site, Amazon also has a variety of steel suppliers.

For more information on Amazon's steel selection, check out my recommendations on DIY Blacksmithing's Toolbox page (diyblacksmith.blogspot.com).

Next Steps Checklist

• Start looking for companies that supply steel near you (this includes scrap yards and large suppliers).

• Think about what you want to make and what type of steel you will use.

• Enjoy the fact that our raw materials are so inexpensive!

CHAPTER THREE:

Forges

For non-blacksmiths, the term 'forge' is a little confusing.

On the one hand, it's the building where a smith does their work.

On the other hand, it's what a smith does: "The smith forges."

On the third hand, the forge is the firebox itself, the glowing heart of the building where all the work happens.

In this chapter, we'll cover the two main types of forges: **coal** and **gas**. We'll talk about the strengths and weaknesses of both and hopefully by the end of it you will have a good idea of which type will work for you.

First, Let's Talk About Fuel

Coal

When it's in its rawest form (never been burned) it's called "green coal." This soft, rock-like material releases a greenish yellow smoke when it's first burned. The smoke is a result of the impurities in the coal burning away.

Green coal is difficult to start a fire with because most of the energy is used to get rid of the impurities. However, this initial burning is a necessary part of the process of converting it into something that is much easier to use: coke.

Coke

Coke is what we want to use to get our fire started. The impurities have been burned away from the green coal so what is left is solid fuel.

As opposed to green coal, which comes in individual rocky chunks, coke often looks lumpy.

This doesn't always hold true so we can rely on two other senses to tell the difference: touch and hearing.

Coke resembles Styrofoam in consistency. Coal is more like rock. When you tap on them or tap them on something, they will respond like these two materials.

And then there's clinker.

Clinker

Clinker gets its name from the sound it makes when you tap it or drop it on something metal like a bucket. It "clinks."

This is what coke becomes when it's all used up. It no longer has any energy-releasing value and should be cleaned out of your firepot.

The biggest reason for this is that it ends up sucking energy out of your fire. This gradually cools it down and works against you as you try to make it hotter.

When you're cleaning out your firepot, clinker is pretty easy to separate out by sight. It takes on crazy deformed shapes and becomes very porous.

Now that we have a better idea about the different stages of coal let's get into coal forges and how you can get one set up over the weekend.

Coal Forges and How to Build One

This forge type has an open flame and burns coal. It requires active fuel management through adding more coal and adjusting airflow with the blower or tuyere.

This is the most popular forge for do-it-yourselfers to build since it doesn't require any welding expertise. It can be done with a barbecue grill, lawnmower deck, or metal sink basin, piping, and a variable speed hair dryer.

Here's a diagram of one set-up:

Coal Forge Setup

Using a barbecue grill, 2" plumbing tee, two threaded nipples, and a blow dryer.

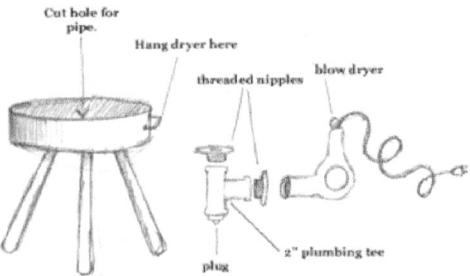

Cut hole for pipe.

Hang dryer here

threaded nipples

blow dryer

2" plumbing tee

plug

© 2014 Ferran Marks

If that diagram isn't clear enough, here is a list of the items you will need:

- One grill, old metal sink, or mower deck minus the motor
- One 2" plumbing tee
- One 2" plumbing plug
- Two 2" threaded plumbing nipples
- One old hairdryer
- A jigsaw to cut a hole in the bottom of the grill

Ideally, you can find a grill with a shallow bottom. Deep grills make it tricky to retrieve pieces of metal when you drop them. For this reason, lawnmower decks are a great choice. They're wide and shallow which also allows for new coal to be banked on the side of the firepot.

Don't worry about a hairdryer with a burned-out heating element. All we need it to do is blow air. We will be making heat with the coal fire.

Pro Tip: Find a blow dryer with a hook on it so you can hang it from the handle of the grill. Adjust it to the appropriate height for your homemade tuyere (piping directing air flow to the forge).

Pro Tip: When you're cutting the hole in the bottom of your grill, make it just big enough for your 2" tee. The threaded nipple goes in from the top to secure the tee to the grill. The plug prevents air from going anywhere but up into your fire.

Lastly, place a fine grate at the bottom of the grill to keep coals and small debris from going into your piping.

Gas Forges – The Easy and Hard Way

Compressed natural gas or propane fuels this forge type. It requires a box or barrel ideally lined with fire bricks or ceramic blanket. To make one yourself you will need welding experience or have a welder for a friend.

The more cost-effective option, in my mind, is to purchase a used forge manufactured by a reputable company. Look for used and new forges on eBay or take a look at blacksmithing forums.

You'll end up spending a lot less time worrying about the strength of your welds and you can get right to work. You also won't be spending a week putting the thing together.

Forges are typically available on eBay from Majestic Forge and Devil Forge out of Lithuania.

If you're dead-set on putting together a gas forge, there are some great videos on YouTube. Here is a list of common materials to use:

- Sheet metal
- Welding equipment
- Piping for the burners
- An igniter
- Fire brick or ceramic blanket
- Tubing and connectors for your fuel source

One method is to simply cut the top and bottom off of a propane cylinder. This saves you the cost of welding equipment and tacking together pieces of sheet metal.

WARNING: If you go this route, make sure that the propane cylinder has been cleaned properly or is brand new and is completely empty.

Grinder Sparks + Fuel = **Unwanted Fire**

Other Considerations

If you live in an area far from coal country, gas may be the most economical fuel type for you. You don't want to pay outrageous prices to ship coal when you have access to natural gas or propane for much less.

For a long time, I just used a 15 lb. propane cylinder to fuel my NC Tool Co. two burner forge. The forge cost around $250 used and the propane was $50 new. It lasted a long time and cost a fraction of that to refill.

Next Steps

- Pick a fuel type.

- Look into the availability of that fuel in your area.

- If you go with coal, start looking around for "firepots." Maybe you have an old push lawnmower that would be put to better use.

- Decide if welding a new firebox is something you want to tackle.

• Brainstorm ideas for airtight boxes for your gas forge.

• Price out your time vs. the cost of a new forge.

CHAPTER FOUR:
The Anvil

Next to the forge, the anvil can be the single most expensive piece of necessary equipment you buy. You have to have something to bang on, though.

In this chapter, I'm going to cover basic terminology, typical anvil cost, and alternatives to dropping a fortune to buy one. By the end of the chapter, you will have some options laid out for you and a better idea of what you want.

Let's start wih **Anvil Anatomy:**

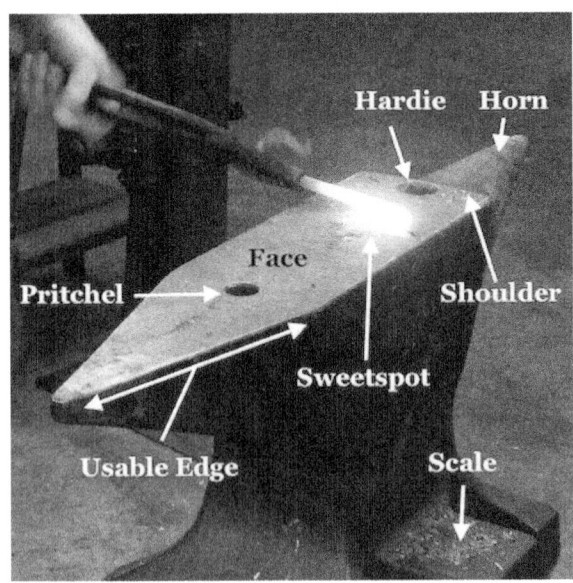

Horn – The most distinctive feature of the traditional anvil, this piece of anatomy is for making curves.

Shoulder or Chipping Block - Used for bends and cutting in combination with a chisel.

Hardie Hole – This hole, often near the shoulder, is square to fit the shanks of a variety of anvil-mounted blacksmith tools such as cutting blocks and swages.

Sweetspot - Believe it or not, this is where the majority of the hammering work gets done. It's about 2 inches by 2 inches just back from the horn and shoulder.

Pritchel Hole - Used for punching jobs and making nails. It allows the thing being punched to drop through.

Usable Edges - The anatomy of an anvil is set up to be utilized. Any and all edges can be used to achieve a task.

Scale - These flaky pieces of metal detach themselves from hot metal during hammering and striking.

Face - This is your workbench and your canvas.

Now that we have some basic anatomy down, let's get into it.

ASOs (Anvil-Shaped Objects)

These are the bane of many blacksmiths' existence. They look like anvils. They're kindof heavy. But they're just not the real thing.

Harbor Freight is well-known for creating anvils that are inexpensive and portable. A true anvil is the exact opposite. You will pay what the anvil is worth and, as a general rule, it should take more than just you to load it into your vehicle.

If you're truly in a pinch, I recommend using some elbow grease on a makeshift anvil.

Makeshift Anvils

Ideally, we could all find an excellent deal on a vintage anvil at a flea market or farm auction. These are both excellent places to look in your area. A variety of anvils are also available on eBay. If you know the size and manufacturer you want, narrowing your search is easy.

Brand new anvils can be too expensive for the blacksmith on a budget. You're looking at $600-800 for the old standard Ridgid/ Peddinghaus and $975 for the base model from a company like Nimba Anvils.

For the frugal blacksmith, there are some inexpensive options out there for makeshift anvils. What you want is that rough shape in a material hard enough and heavy enough to take the blows of your hammer.

That hardness and heaviness is necessary because as you're hammering a piece of steel, you're actually working it from two sides at once. The anvil is shaping it at the same time as the hammer.

My top choice for a makeshift anvil is a piece of railroad track. After talking with an experienced smith down in the mountains of North Carolina, he was willing to give me an old section of track. I cleaned it up and used it to forge countless hooks and fire tools.

The piece he gave me is 18" long and about 6" tall. It doesn't have the standard and hardie or pritchel holes, but for a blacksmith just starting out, it does the job.

I used it for years pounding on the top of the track. However, in my research I found that a lot of smiths were flipping the track on its end and using the side of the rail.

They would mount it on a piece of wood in this position for stability and to distribute the downward forces. For more on this method, check out AnvilFire.com's article: **Tools from RR Rail**.

Where to Source Railroad Track

If you're looking for a piece of track, eBay always has sellers. You can have one for very little money. There are some sellers who even offer to cut it to length for you.

Railroad suppliers are another place to look. They might not have the length you want, though. To save on shipping costs, it's better to find a local supplier and go down in person.

I-Beams

Another idea is to look up your local steel supplier and see if they have I-beams for sale. The advantage of the I-beam is that it has a wide, flat face that can be drilled out to create your hardie and pritchel holes. It's also good and heavy.

To mount it, you could either drill out the base if you have the right tools for the job, bend nails over the base or, if it has holes, use a chain like I did for my Quick Mount Anvil on the next page.

One thing to consider about I-beams is that they have a slender web (the vertical part connecting the flat flanges). This may not distribute the force of your hammer blows very evenly leading to an overly bouncy face.

You want to get the most bang for your buck when you're directing your blows. Having your piece and your hammer bounce around is inefficient.

The Final Word on Makeshift Anvils

For the money, about $30 as I write this, a piece of railroad track will suit your needs just fine. If you have an itch for tinkering, you can modify your piece of track with grinders, cutting torches, and welding equipment to create a horn and a more typical anvil shape.

Anvil Size

When it comes to anvils, bigger and heavier is generally better. The heavier the anvil is the better it will withstand the amount of work you want to do with it.

Weight is important. You don't want to hammer on large bar stock with a small 40 lb. anvil below it. You'll wear out the anvil in a hurry.

Here are some guidelines:

- 40 lb. anvil: Use ¼" stock or smaller.
- 50 – 100 lb. anvils: Up to 1" stock.
- 150 lb. anvils and up: Use these bigger guys for stock larger than 1 ½".

A Quick Note on Anvil Height

To save your elbows and your back, spend a few minutes measuring your anvil height. Follow these steps and you'll be golden:

1. With your arms at your sides, make a fist.

2. Using a tape measure, find the distance from the floor to the knuckles of your clenched fist.

3. This where the top of your anvil should be. When it's set on its stand or stump, the knuckles of your striking hand should rest on its face.

Next Steps

- In the U.S. look at Craigslist for anvils in your area. You can type in "anvils" in the left hand search box and select 'For Sale.' You might be surprised.

- Scout out railroad track on eBay.

- Don't buy an ASO if you can avoid it.

- Get creative. What other items are available to you that you could use as an anvil? I've seen Ethiopian blacksmiths use a claw hammer and a rock to forge steel. That's the type of ingenuity I love!

CHAPTER FIVE:

Hammers and Tongs

So you have an anvil, a forge, and a place where you can be as loud as you want. Now you need the hand tools.

In this chapter, We'll go over different types of hammers and tongs, the types I use, and where to get them.

Hammers

If you read the Next Steps Checklist at the end of the last chapter, you may have noticed my comment about Ethiopian smiths using a claw hammer and a rock to work metal.

A 16 oz. claw hammer is a little light for the work we want to do and you'll end up leaving crescent-shaped dings in the metal, but you could do it. However, as blacksmiths we use a particular type of hammer.

What's a Cross Peen?

I recommend investing $30 in a legitimate blacksmith's cross peen hammer. The hammer I have used for years is pictured above. You'll notice that instead of two flat faces like a sledge hammer or a face and a ball like a ball peen hammer, it tapers to a horizontal line at the back.

This is the "cross" peen. It's used for spreading metal in two directions rather than all directions like the hammer's face.

Hammer Shapes by Country

The cross peen I'm using as our example is a 2 ½ lb. Nordic-style hammer. This isn't the only shape a blacksmith's hammer can take. Many countries around the world have their own distinct style of hammer. The French style is slightly different from the German which is different from the Swedish. They're all different from the Hofi.

Note: For examples of all of these visit blacksmithsupply.com.

The Hofi-style ergonomic hammer is a departure from the classic style. The weight of the head is more centralized to be easier on the elbows. With the amount of hammering we do, any protection from wear-and-tear is welcome.

The Hofi hammer sells for $100+ and is generally not something I recommend to new smiths. If you decide to get one in the future I'm sure your blacksmith's elbow will thank you.

Tongs

When dealing with temperatures over 1500 degrees Fahrenheit, you need to extend your reach. That's what a good set of tongs will do for you.

There are a lot of different kinds of tongs. Tongs for shoeing horses, tongs for forging rings, tongs for scrollwork...

The best set of all-around tongs can be found at Blacksmith Supply. They're called bolt style Tom Tongs. You can hold both square and round stock with them and they feel good in your hand.

A set of ½″ Tom Tongs will run you $40. That's $40 well-spent.

Next Steps

- Decide on your hammer style.

- Pick out a pair of tongs.

- Create your workspace!

CHAPTER SIX:

Creating Your Workspace

Blacksmiths are loudest when they're not talking. This makes it a difficult trade for close neighbors. If you live in town or at the end of a cul-de-sac, you might have to find an alternative place to do your forging.

One of the best places I've set up shop was an open-air shed at least a few blocks away from the nearest residence. It had everything I needed underneath a solid, corrugated steel roof. The walls weren't insulated, but I managed to keep warm with the forge and my hammering.

In this chapter, I'm going to show you a simple set-up you can do in an afternoon if you haven't convinced your significant other/ roommates/parents to let you use the garage.

Open-Air Forging

Between the anvil, the forge, and the quenching tub, blacksmiths don't need a lot of space to work. Their main obstacle is usually other people.

While other folks find the process of forging iron and steel fascinating, they want to experience it on their own terms. They want to go *somewhere* to see it done rather than have it going on next door.

This is how I set up a quick shop in the backyard when I was first starting. It took me less than a day.

Step 1: Select Your Space

I chose a piece of mostly flat ground at the edge of the backyard. I measured it out square at 10 feet by 10 feet. The thought here is to give yourself plenty of room to position your stump for the anvil, your forge set-up, and your quenching tub. You also want to be able to move freely between these stations.

The bonus was that the site I picked overlooks the pond on the property next to us.

Step 2: Gathering Materials

A few things you might want to have:

• Concrete blocks to use as a foundation for your forge stand.
• A hoe or other grubbing tool to remove grass and plant life for fireproofing (pieces of hot metal and sparks tend to fly).
• Stone to line your area. Without walls it's nice to define the space with a boundary.
• Tape measure. Spacing the concrete blocks properly will save some headaches. You'll also need it for setting the height of your anvil.

Step 3: Setting the Foundations

Measure the width between the legs of your forge stand or small table.

Dig out two holes, each the proper size to hold your concrete blocks. When you have them in the ground they should be level with the top of the dirt.

This photo may explain it better:

Step 4: Stump-setting

Your anvil needs a place to sit. I recommend using a section of hardwood set into the ground.

For my set-up, I was able to get my hands on a piece of hickory. It had recently fallen on its own so I cut off a piece that was 5 feet 6 inches long.

One thing I didn't fully account for when I selected it is the diameter of the log. It ended up being a little less than the length of my railroad track anvil. Ideally, you want the diameter to match or be greater than the longest part of the anvil base.

However, since this was a found piece of wood, I was happy to make it work.

A Little Stump History

Blacksmiths throughout history have used green (just downed or recently fallen) hardwood stumps for anvil mounts. Hickory is a good choice because of its weight and density. It takes the blows sent from the hammer through the anvil well.

Note: If hickory isn't available in your area, other hardwoods will do: Oak, Maple, Poplar, Walnut.

Traditionally, the blacksmith would set the stump between 4 and 5 feet into the ground after doing some careful measurement. This was to ensure that the height of the stump complemented his own.

Adding the 4-5 feet in the ground to the 4 feet above ground, you end up trying to maneuver a very long, heavy piece of wood. For our setup, we won't be going that far.

Anvil Height

I mentioned it earlier, but I'd like to go into greater detail about anvil height. The **general rule for anvil height** is to have the face of your anvil meet the knuckles of your clenched fist when it's held at your side. This prevents you from putting strain on your elbow and back while hammering.

For example, my personal measurement from the ground to my fist is about 33 inches. This will vary more due to arm length and leg length than overall height, but for reference I'm 6'1''.

Accounting for the 6 1/4" height of my piece of railroad track and the 12 inches of stump going into the ground, I had to cut my piece of hickory down some. To do this I used a chainsaw, but bow saws or single-buck crosscut saws can do the job just fine.

Just remember, **the ending height with the anvil resting on the stump needs to equal your knuckle to ground measurement**.

Step 5: Defining the Area

Using stone as a border and gravel as a floor, you can create a defined, fireproof space for your shop.

I used a flat-headed shovel to dig out the border of my 10' x 10' forging area. It was just a simple 'V' trench wide enough to hold the stones and rubble I collected from under the house.

Step 6: Everything In Its Right Place

As you may have noticed in the photograph, I set a second section of hickory into the ground. I used it to mount a small bench vise. I clamped my U-bar in it to bend my mild steel blanks into hooks.

I also used that stump to hold my miniature quenching can. You don't need a giant barrel to have an effective quenching tub. I used an empty bean can for mine.

CHAPTER SEVEN:

Finishes

Now that you have your space set up and you've been tinkering with metal for a while, what's next? To keep it from rusting you'll need to seal it somehow.

In this chapter, we'll talk about a few options for finishing a piece steel.

TRADITIONAL

Traditional finishing methods rely on natural rather than artificial substances to seal the metal. This is metal preservation in its simplest form.

Beeswax

I use beeswax almost exclusively to seal my pieces. It's natural and gives the metal a nice, darker look.

Here are the steps I use to seal a piece with beeswax:

1. Holding the piece with tongs, heat the steel with a propane torch or place it in your forge. It should take just a few seconds to reach the proper heat to melt the beeswax. You don't want it to glow. It just has to be hot enough to melt the wax.

2. Still holding the metal with the tongs, lightly rub it with a bar of beeswax, turning it to coat the entire piece. It should be melting on contact and dripping. If it's making flames, the metal is too hot. Don't panic. Just blow it out

and let it cool for a couple
seconds. Then reapply.

3. When the piece is covered, wipe
    off the excess wax with a rag. I
    like to use old t-shirts. The jersey
    cotton absorbs the extra wax
    really well.

4. At this point the piece of steel is still
    very hot, so set it aside using the
    tongs. It will take a few minutes
    for it to cool down.

5. Be sure to set it aside on something
    that is not flammable. The risk is
    pretty low that it will catch fire,
    but it's better to be sure.

Beeswax, Linseed Oil, and Turpentine

Some smiths prefer a mixture of beeswax,
linseed oil, and turpentine to seal their pieces.
The benefit of this method is that once the
mixture liquefies, it can be applied smoothly
with a brush. This makes it easier to seal more
items in less time.

You can melt the ingredients together in a process similar to this one:

1. Slowly heat the ingredients in a large metal pot or crock.

2. After you have heated your piece in your forge or with a propane torch, brush on the mixture. You will then wipe off the excess liquid with a rag and set it aside to cool.

Things you will need:

- An unused paintbrush
- A pot you don't plan to cook with anymore.
- A rag
- ½ lb. of beeswax
- 1 quart of linseed oil
- 1 quart of turpentine

Note: You won't need to use all of the beeswax, linseed oil, and turpentine. I recommend some experimentation to find the right mixture for you.)

Make Mine Black

Have you ever wondered how traditionally forged ironwork gets that deep black look? The following process will show you how.

You can use either of the above methods for sealing the metal, but before wiping off the extra wax, **smoke the piece**.

Here's how:

1. Start a smoky, green (fresh) coal fire. This is coal that has not been burned and has not released its impurities. You want those impurities for this to work. *Note: If you would rather not breathe in coal fumes or you are using a gas forge, you can also start a smoky fire with small twigs and green leaves.*

2. The key here is to produce smoke.

3. After heating the piece with a torch or in the forge, apply the beeswax or turpentine mixture.

4. When it's fully coated and still dripping, use the tongs to turn it and wave it in the sooty smoke of the fire. This will blacken the metal.

5. Wipe away the extra wax and soot. Your metal will come out with a deep, dark finish.

MODERN FINISHING TECHNIQUES

These methods are generally faster and involve less labor, but the results can be less desirable depending on your preferences.

Paint

The quickest and surest way to seal a piece and protect it against rust is to paint it. An evenly applied coat of paint will prevent metal from rusting for years if not decades.

There *is* a downside to coating your pieces this way. Flashy paint colors or textures tend to take away from the handmade quality of a piece. All of those cool dimples, hammer strokes, and minor flaws are almost completely erased when paint is applied.

If you choose to paint your metal, I recommend glossy or matte black spray paint. This will retain most of the raw metal's characteristics.

To preserve the metal's original look and texture, but still seal it, consider clear matte finish spray paint. This is an excellent way to show off the metal's natural qualities.

Rustoleum and Krylon both have high-quality, inexpensive options for spray-on coatings.

Pro Tip: I recommend wearing a dust mask and spraying in a well-ventilated area. The chemicals they use in these paints and coatings aren't particularly friendly to your brain and lungs.

Powder Coating

One of the coolest ways to cover just about anything, powder coating is most often used in industrial settings. It coats evenly and is extremely durable.

The downside is that it removes all the marks of your craftsmanship and leaves you with something you could buy at a store. I'm not against powder coating. I love it, but it's not practical for this ancient art.

ADVANCED FINISHING TECHNIQUES

There are some projects that will require more advanced techniques. Knives, punches, and chisels all come to mind. For these items you will need an understanding of hardening and tempering.

Hardening and Tempering

Hardening and tempering could have their own large section, but I'll hit the basics here. These two techniques are used for heat-treating metal to be used as tools.

First you harden. Then you temper. The most common application these days is with knife making.

Hardening in 6 Steps

1. Fill a large metal tub or pot with either used motor oil (this flames up pretty good) or linseed oil and turpentine. It should be deep enough to submerge your piece and wide enough to move it in circles and figure eights.

2. Take your fully forged piece and set it in your preheated forge (both gas and coal forges can be used.)

3. Have a long magnet handy to test magnetism periodically.

4. When your piece of steel is glowing cherry red, touch the long magnet to it. If it's magnetic, put it in the forge for an additional 5 seconds then test again.

5. If it's no longer magnetic (there's no attraction between the metal and the magnet), quench it in the metal tub with the oil in it. Quenching at this point will cause the molecules of the metal to seize in their hardened configuration.

6. I recommend swirling it in figure eights or back to front to ensure that it's evenly quenched.

*To see this in action, check out The DIY Blacksmithing Online Course at diyblacksmithing.teachable.com.

Tempering in 3 Steps

1. Tempering is a gradual, low heat softening of the metal. This allows for hardness and the ability to sharpen the blade. *Note: If you try to sharpen a blade that has only been*

hardened, you'll wear your arms out before you make much progress. The file will slide off without removing any metal.

2. Paying close attention and with the sharp side of the blade pointed away from the heat source, slowly heat the knife to blue (600 degrees Fahrenheit/315 degrees centigrade) at the spine and straw-colored at the blade edge (approximately 400-450 degrees Fahrenheit, 260 C). This softens the spine more than the blade edge which you want to stay hard.

3. Quench it with the figure-eight motion as you used to harden it. This locks in the temper. Once it cools completely, the cutting edge can now be sharpened and still retain its hardness and durability.

Next Steps:

• Try out a few of the techniques we talked about and see which ones you like.

• Pick up a can of clear matte finish and a block of beeswax and compare the results.

• Learn more about all things blacksmithing at diyblacksmithing.teachable.com.

Bonus Chapter:
Business for Blacksmiths

What was once the cornerstone of the village became a hobby with the development of machines. We have come full-circle to seeing blacksmithing become a sought-after profession once again.

If you have ever entertained the idea of working with your hands, creating functional art this chapter is for you. In it I'll provide you with the basic components you will need to start a blacksmithing business. We'll talk about what sells, who buys it, and where to sell it.

What Sells?

Architectural iron gates.

Just kidding.

While there *is* a market for large iron gates, it's not where I would suggest you start. A more accessible category to target is **useful, everyday items**.

Of the many different things I have forged over the years, the thing that has sold the most is hooks. There's nothing particularly special or ornate about the hooks I make either. They are your average hand-forged hooks to hold up handbags, towels, coats, etc.

When I was learning how to forge, I was told by a few of my teachers about the importance of "bread and butter" ironwork. Hooks fall squarely into this category. They're generally inexpensive (for you to make and the customer to buy) and extremely useful.

Customers will appreciate the handmade touch of a forged hook as well as the low cost of having it in their home. They'll be happy to spend $30 for a set of 3 hooks as opposed to $10,000 - $20,000 for an iron gate. You can always work your way up to laying out those awesome gates for them in the future. Your hooks or other everyday items are a great foot in the door.

*For more on forging and selling hooks, check out **Hooks 101: How to Make $99 an Hour**.

Who Buys Ironwork?

Everybody! The sad fact is that they often end up buying manufactured ironwork instead of handmade items. Their coat racks are made in a factory somewhere that makes thousands of identical coat racks. They don't have any character or individuality.

That's where we blacksmiths come in. Wouldn't it be great if they bought something unique from you instead of something everyone else has?

Where Do I Sell My Stuff?

So you have some hooks you've made or maybe you got ambitious and started forging knives. Now you have to get it in front of people.

The great news is that you have more options than ever these days. In this section we'll talk about where to sell your goods both online and off.

Online

In the past 10 years, Etsy has become an excellent venue for selling blacksmith goods. People flock to the site to buy handmade items. They are especially interested in one-of-a-kind items for their homes.

It seems like customers nowadays would rather have unique, high quality items made by people they have interacted with personally. That's one of the greatest benefits of Etsy – you can communicate with the person buying from you very easily.

Offline

When it comes to selling what you've made in person, your local farmers market is an excellent place to start. The cost to put up a booth is usually very reasonable especially compared to the rent on shop space.

You will likely be surrounded by a variety of different goods including produce, soaps, candles, and woodworking. While this may seem too busy, it's actually to your advantage as a metalworker. Your particular craft will stand out from the carved gnomes and giant zucchinis.

Festivals are another good option for selling what you've made. Festivalnet.com is a great resource for finding out about what festivals are coming up and where. If you like to travel, you can hit up a festival every weekend.

The last suggestion I'll give for offline sales is to open your own store. There are positives and negatives to this, but I would caution against it when you're just starting out.

The Negatives

- Overhead can be expensive before you have even turned a profit. You have to cover rent and utilities without knowing if your location is the right one.

- Foot traffic alone in a medium-sized town is not guaranteed to keep you afloat.

- You need to be where the buyers are. People are making their purchases online more and more.

The Positive

The greatest thing about having your own shop is the in-person relationships you can build with customers. People like to touch and feel ironwork and being able to walk in and do that is one of the most effective selling tactics out there.

Next Steps

Hopefully this introduction to the world of owning and operating a blacksmithing business has given you some ideas for getting started. To cover everything involved would fill up its own book.

A Final Word and One Last Step

Thanks for picking up The DIY Blacksmithing Book! Hopefully, you now have some inspiration and actionable steps to take to start forging.

If this book was helpful to you, please leave a kind review on Amazon. By leaving a positive review you make it easier for aspiring blacksmiths to find good information. Help spread the word!

Thank you!

Other works by the Author:

- **The DIY Blacksmithing Online Course** - diyblacksmithing.teachable.com

This course is open to anyone with an interest in learning more about blacksmithing without investing a lot of money up front. Open enrollment.

- Hooks 101: How To Make $99 An Hour

- U.S. Blacksmith Schools - Find a Blacksmithing Class Near You

- The 2019 Anvil and Forge Buying Guide

- DIY Knife Making - Bushcraft Knives

About the Author

TERRAN MARKS IS A professional blacksmith and writer who, like Vulcan, spends most of his time working with a silent intensity.

He teaches **online blacksmithing classes** at **diyblacksmithing.teachable.com** and in-person at Brown County Forge.

He can also often be found hiking in the wilds of North America.

Printed in Great Britain
by Amazon

70199579R00041